A CALL TO

God's Daughters

TO STEP INTO HIS L.A.B

LOVE   ACCEPTANCE   BEAUTY

BASED ON THE BOOK OF RUTH

KRISTA PETTIFORD

MAKK PUBLISHING CO

SAN DIEGO, CA

Printed in the United States of America.

This publication is not intended to provide professional advice. It is sold with the understanding that neither the author nor the publisher is engaged in rendering health, medical, or other professional services.

For more information: MAKK Publishing Co. 772 Jamacha Rd, El Cajon CA, 92019 ISBN 978-0-9823805-5-0

Library of Congress Control Number: 2015921293

CONTENTS

This book is dedicated to all of God's Daughters. Thank you, Lord, for entrusting me with the assignment to make known what it means to be loved, accepted, and beautiful in the eyes of our Heavenly Father.

PREFACE

THIS BOOK WAS INSPIRED by another book I wrote entitled *Prettiful, Changing the Garments of Your Heart.* When I began writing the book, I thought I was headed in the right direction, but the closer I came to completing Prettiful, the more uneasy I felt about it.

Even though I believed the book shared a relevant message and was written in a way that I felt would have encouraged women to step into their identity in Christ, I was growing uncertain about whether or not God wanted me to publish it.

I tried to press through and finish the book, but the more I tried to write, the harder it was and the clearer the voice of the Holy Spirit became.

When I finally gave Him my full attention, I heard Him saying what I knew all along. I had to surrender the book. He did not want me to finish it or publish it.

I still pressed on to finish the book, hoping I could somehow talk God into it. I went as far as sending it to my editor. I had already told people the book would be out and shared the book cover. I explained all this to the Lord, but He still said no.

At the time, I could not understand why God would not allow me to go forward with the book, but I am thankful that He did not give up. Nevertheless, during my prayer time, and every time I started to write or talk about the book, an uneasy feeling would come up in my spirit.

Finally, I told the Lord I would give up the book, and I did. I gave it up as much as my heart could bear. But I held onto the hope that He might let me finish and publish the book one day.

When I finally accepted God's answer, I did not try to explain anything to people because I knew they wouldn't understand. I just stopped talking about it.

Then I attended the Declare Conference for Christian bloggers in Dallas, Texas. On the first day of the conference, a speaker shared a similar testimony to mine: I laughed and cried. It was like she was telling my story, and I had been sent there to hear the real reason God had told me "no."

She said a book she had written started as a God-project too, but soon it became her project. It became about building a platform for her, not an altar for God. God asked her to surrender her book too. However, He gave her another one that led to her being asked to speak at Declare. I can sum up her whole message in four words:

" *Build altars, not platforms.*"

I was guilty of trying to build a platform for myself through my book. I did not see it like this until I heard her story, but I could not deny that I had lost sight of why I was writing Prettiful. It was no longer about God.

Before the next speaker, the worship team came, and a young woman with a beautiful voice sang what became one of my favorite songs, an original called *"Satisfy."* As she sang about how the Lord satisfies our every longing, I remembered that He truly satisfies my soul and is enough.

With tears running down my face, I let go of the book. I surrendered the right to bring it back up to the Lord or to try and find a reason to publish it. That was my promise to God, and I kept it.

In that same moment, the Holy Spirit spoke clearly in my heart. He told me to take the three main points that Prettiful was based on and write another book. To be exact, I heard Him say, *"Call My Daughters into My L.A.B. — My love, acceptance, and beauty."* He then began to give me the outline for the book.

The amazing thing is that as soon as I surrendered what I was holding onto, not knowing what was next, and decided to trust God, He gave me what He had been holding for me. I firmly believe that if you build an altar for God's people through the work he calls you to do, He will build your platform.

During that time, I was not so coincidentally reading the story of Ruth in the fictional book, *A Lineage of Grace: Five Women of Unlikely Heritage Who Changed Eternity* by Francine Rivers. I noticed the parallels to God's love, acceptance, and beauty in Ruth's life and her relationships with Naomi and Boaz.

As the Lord began to show me what to share with you, He told me to study Ruth's story. Her story is the perfect example of what it's like to step into God's love, acceptance, and beauty. I am thankful that I laid aside what I had so I could receive what God had for me, something worthy of giving to you. With a surrendered and satisfied heart, I write to you, daughter of God, on behalf of your Father.

INTRODUCTION

WHATEVER DIFFERENCES WE HAVE, all women have three things in common: a desire to experience genuine love, a desire to be accepted for who we really are, and a desire to feel beautiful.

At the core of these desires is the inborn image of God within us. He is love, He is the grantor of eternal acceptance, and He is the Beautiful One.

As women, what we believe about love, acceptance, and beauty is significant to every other aspect of our lives, our mindsets – the attitudes and opinions that form our thought processes. Our standards – the measure we use to judge ourselves and others and make decisions, and our ability to fulfill our mission – God's purpose for our lives, are all affected by what we believe about love, acceptance, and beauty.

As God's daughters, we are supposed to find and define love, acceptance, and beauty in Him *first* and then lead our lives based on the truth of His word.

In Christ, He's given us everything we need to do just that. He put His love in our hearts so we can give and receive love as He does. He's already accepted us in the Beloved, so we don't have to seek man's acceptance at the cost of diminishing ourselves. He created us in His image, with His beauty, so we can be confident in how we look and show up in the world.

Unfortunately, in this day of social media and reality T.V., too many of God's daughters have allowed their thinking to be influenced by the world's definitions of love, acceptance, and beauty. As a result, their God-given desires are not realized in a healthy way.

This isn't God's plan. He didn't design us to conform to the world's standards but to be transformed by renewing our minds. To know that we are completely loved, accepted, and beautifully and wonderfully created by Him. To believe that we are worthy of genuine love and acceptance from others without pretense and that our beauty is defined by more than our clothes, body types, make-up, or hair. If we don't believe God loves us, we will approach Him through religion instead of a relationship. We won't believe He cares enough about us to care what happens to us personally. We won't believe that He wants what's best for us or that He wants to answer our prayers and fulfill the desires of our hearts.

If we don't believe God accepts us because of His grace, we will try to earn His acceptance instead of simply stepping into it.

If we don't learn to accept ourselves with all our imperfections and feel secure in who we are, we will always strive to be more, do more, and have more to feel worthy. We will constantly compare ourselves to others and never be content with who we are

> **If we don't believe that God loves us, we will approach Him through religion instead of relationship.**

and what we have. We will never see ourselves as worthy of total acceptance from others without feeling the need to pretend, if necessary, to be what they expect of us until we understand what it means to be accepted by God. We will compromise our identity in Christ to gain the acceptance of people.

If we don't believe that we are beautiful without all the pretense and pomp, we will focus on outer beauty and never learn to nurture the beauty in our hearts.

The truth is that many women have known love, been accepted, and felt beautiful. Unfortunately, too many women have never truly experienced the fullness of God's love, acceptance, and beauty at work in their lives.

Ruth's story illustrates what it's like to experience the fullness of God's love, acceptance, and beauty through not only the good seasons but the difficult seasons of life.

Dear Daughter

I AM calling you to step fully in My love, acceptance, and beauty so you can become the woman I created you to be, triumph through every season, and reach your destiny.

YOUR FATHER,

FROM THE LOINS OF LOT

RUTH was a Moabitess, a descendant of Lot, Abraham's nephew. Abraham took Lot with him when he left Ur to follow God by faith (see Genesis 12). However, Lot moved to Sodom when he and Abraham's men fought over land for their cattle (Genesis 13).

In Sodom, the people did so much wickedness the Lord destroyed the entire city with the people in it in one day. But Lot was righteous and became miserable with all the sin around him. The New Testament says, God:

> Rescued righteous Lot, greatly distressed by the sensual conduct of the wicked (for as that righteous man lived among them day after day, he was tormenting his righteous soul over their law-less deeds that he saw and heard); then the Lord knows how to rescue the godly from trials. (2 Peter 2:7-8)

When the Lord got ready to destroy Sodom, He ensured Lot was out of the city on the eve of its destruction. But Lot's wife looked back at the town after the angels warned them not to, and she turned into a pillar of salt, leaving Lot alone with their two daughters. Then Lot and his daughters fled to the mountains of Zoar together (read Genesis chapter 19).

When they arrived, the oldest daughter devised a plan to get Lot drunk and take turns having sex with him to "preserve their father's lineage." They did, and both sisters got pregnant.

> *The firstborn bore a son and called his name Moab; he is the father of the Moabites. The younger also bore a son and called his name Ben-Ammi. He is the father of the Ammonites to this day. (Genesis 19:37-38)*

Even though Lot's daughters did this wicked thing, the Lord still loved Lot.

I believe Lot's family was greatly influenced by evil and ungodly practices while living in Sodom. Eventually, Lot's descendants turned entirely from the true God of their father and worshiped the idol god Chemosh. They fought with all the people around them, including the children of Israel. Through all this, the Lord still honored Lot's faith in Him, and his descendants continued to commit transgressions against God.

When the children of Israel traveled through the wilderness, the Lord warned Moses not to bother the Moabites. *"Then the Lord said to me, 'Do not harass Moab, nor contend with them in battle, for I will not give you any of their lands as a possession because I have given Ar to the de-scendants of Lot as a possession' " (Deuteronomy 2:9).*

Even though the Lord commanded the children of Israel not to bother the Moabites, they still tried to have the children of Israel cursed by one of their prophets, but God would not allow it.

After many plots to destroy Israel by the Moabites and their brother nation, the Ammonites, the Lord vowed against them all:

> *An Ammonite or Moabite shall not enter the assembly of the Lord; even to the tenth generation none of his descendants shall enter the assembly of the Lord, because they did not meet you with bread and water on the road when you came out of Egypt, and because they hired against you Balaam the son of Beor from Pethor of Mesopotamia, to curse you. (Deuteronomy 23:3-4)*

Ruth was born under that curse, but by grace, through Ruth's faith, the Lord wrote Lot back into His story because he had gone with Abraham by faith, believing God.

Using the genealogy of Jesus in Matthew 1 and Luke 3, you can see that Ruth's birth came before the tenth generation, even though the Lord vowed against the Moabites not to allow them into His assembly.

Though some scholars say that the rules were different for men than women, the Lord clearly said "none of the descendants," which would include women.

God honored Ruth's faith and, by grace, drew her to Himself. Ruth's righteousness broke the curse over her life. She was allowed among His people and became part of His family.

Ruth's story is one of breaking a generational curse, claiming a lost inheritance, and becoming the woman God created her to

> *Ruth's story is one of breaking a generational curse, claiming a lost inheritance and becoming the woman God created her to be.*

be. Not only did Ruth step into God's love, acceptance, and beauty, but she took back the inheritance Lot's daughters lost when they took matters into their own hands and turned from the Living God.

Maybe you come from a long line of people who do not serve the Lord. Perhaps you've been in a spiritual Moab, where darkness surrounds you, but you have a heart for God. Jesus has already done the work of breaking the curse from you. God is calling you to walk away from who you were and what you once knew, step into your new identity, and claim your inheritance as His daughter.

A DAUGHTER OF DESTINY

THERE IS A FRIEND WHO STICKS CLOSER THAN A
BROTHER.
(PROVERBS 18:24)

RUTH'S name means friend or neighbor. Her story starts when she marries for the first time, and Naomi, her mother-in-law, is already a widow living in a foreign land. Ruth was married for about ten years, so she must have be-come close to her mother-in-law.

Ruth's first husband was Mahlon; his name means sickness, and his brother Chilion's name means destruction. In Biblical times, Hebrew names had a specific prophetic meaning which often foretold the person's destiny.

When a famine came, Mahlon and Chilion left Bethlehem with their parents to live in Moab.

With names like sickness and destruction and the fact that they left without God's instruction, it's fair to assume that Mahlon and Chilion weren't men who followed the Lord with their whole hearts.

Both sons met their wives in Moab and later died like their father, leaving Ruth and Orpah at a disadvantage as young widows. Naomi had little hope of obtaining her inheritance back in Bethlehem as a widow with no sons (see Ruth chapter 1).

After Naomi's sons died in Moab, she decided to go back home to Bethlehem but told her daughters-in-law to return to their families, be with their mothers, and find new husbands.

However, Ruth refused to leave her mother-in-law. With defiant faith, she insisted on going with Naomi back to Bethlehem. She was willing to leave everything she knew and go to a foreign land.

The question is why.

I believe it was because something was missing from Ruth's life, something she couldn't put her finger on, but she knew it wasn't in Moab with her family or in finding a new husband.

Ruth had seen glimpses of what it was like to experience not just a man's love but God's love, acceptance, and beauty through her mother-in-law. She had the opportunity to witness Naomi's relationship with God during the years they spent together while her husband was still alive.

She witnessed Naomi hold onto her faith through the most bitter season of her life and cling to this God who she believed loved her, accepted her, and called her beautiful when her sons died after she had already lost her husband.

She witnessed Naomi's desire to return to the place where she came to know her God. All these things ignited Ruth's desire to know the one true God for herself.

The seed of faith in Ruth had been sown and watered by Naomi's life. As God's daughter, Ruth wanted to experience love, acceptance, and beauty. She knew this would never happen if she stayed in Moab. Besides, she felt it was her turn to encourage Naomi's faith.

Ruth's story is not primarily about meeting Boaz, though he played a significant role in God's plan for her life. Ruth's story is one of believing and becoming.

By faith, Ruth believed God would be her God and take care of her with all the love, acceptance, and beauty He showered on Naomi, and He did.

Boaz was Ruth's door to her destiny. He was her sweet reward for being satisfied with the Lord as her portion and keeping a pleasant and hopeful attitude throughout a long season of suffering and sacrifice.

Ruth completely gave her life to God, and she tasted His goodness. He proved beyond any shadow of a doubt the depths and richness of His love for her. He proved the favor that follows being accepted by Him, and the benefits of allowing His beauty to be demonstrated through a yielded heart were worth infinitely more than all she left behind.

God is no respecter of persons. What He did for Ruth, He will do for you. He loves us all the same. He accepts everyone who calls upon His name and places His beauty inside our hearts. But we must be willing to leave behind who we were and step fully into our new identity.

To take a step means to move—lifting the foot and setting it down again in a new position, accompanied by shifting the body's weight in the direction of the new position. God wants you to lift yourself from where you are and shift the weight of your faith in the direction of your destiny as His daughter.

The following pages contain a summary of your inheritance, an opportunity to see yourself in Ruth's story and be encouraged to change how your story ends. Maybe you've already met your Boaz, and perhaps you haven't.

Perhaps you are already married. Maybe God has a Boaz ready to be written into your story, and maybe not. I will leave writing your story to you and God. But I can promise you this: God has a good plan for you and a beautiful inheritance waiting for you.

Beloved, my prayer is that as we look at the promises of God to His daughters and the parallels found in Ruth's story, you will be inspired to step fully into God's L.A.B., obtain your inheritance, and be who He created you to be.

MEET NAOMI

He has made everything beautiful in its time. Also, He has put eternity in their hearts, except that no one can find out the work that God does from beginning to end. (Ecclesiastes 3:11)

If you don't feel beautiful inside, if your circumstances make you feel bitter at times, if your attitude doesn't always reflect the woman you know God called you to be, I pray that Naomi's story will encourage you.

Naomi was married to an Ephrathite from Bethlehem, Judah, named Elimelech. They had two sons – Mahlon and Chilion. Elimelech relocated his family to Moab because a famine hit the land of Bethlehem. The Bible never says that the Lord told him to do so. In fact, many people stayed in Bethlehem during the famine and survived.

Soon after they arrived, Elimelech died, leaving Naomi alone with her two sons. After their father died, instead of returning to Bethlehem, both sons married Moabite women—Orpah and

Ruth—but after about ten years, both men died without having any children.

Around the same time her sons died, Naomi heard the famine had ended in Bethlehem, so she decided to return. Though she had gone out full with a family, health, and wealth, she was going back empty, with no money and no family.

The Lord had let her live but allowed her sons and husband to die, leaving her without a grandson who could one day provide for her. She felt the Lord had dealt harshly with her and that He brought calamity upon her.

Naomi's name means pleasant, a word associated with Godly beauty. However, when she returned to Bethlehem, she asked people to call her Mara, which comes from the Hebrew word bitter, which means to be angry, irritated, unhappy and weighed down (see Ruth 1:20).

Although Naomi was going through an unpleasant time in her life and felt bitter, God never called her Mara. Naomi called herself Mara because she allowed her situation to overshadow her God-given identity. Nevertheless, Naomi was still beautiful in the eyes of the Lord.

You cannot reflect the Lord's beauty while holding onto bitterness. Even when we wallow in the bitterness of our circumstances and develop unpleasant attitudes, the Lord sees beyond our bitterness. He sees the inner beauty hidden behind the scars and the brokenness in our hearts.

> *You cannot reflect the beauty of the Lord while you hold onto bitterness.*

Though God makes everything beautiful, even things that seem at first to be ugly, we must be willing to let God's work reveal their beauty over time.

Naomi's breakthrough came because she chose to move forward despite her bitterness and brokenness. She left the place where she became bitter and returned to the place where her life with the Lord began: the place where she received her name, had a pleasant life, and came to know the Lord's love, acceptance, and beauty.

She was still bitter when she made it back to Bethlehem. But because she had moved on from the place of her tragedies, she could let go of her past and accept her losses. She could process what happened through the lens of God's goodness. She started her life over again.

When Naomi began focusing on helping others, mainly doing what she could to secure a future for her daughter-in-law Ruth, she was able to let go of the bitterness and gain hope for their future.

Naomi had to decide to be pleasant despite what had happened to her. She chose beauty over bitterness. As soon as she focused on the blessings before her instead of the pain of her past, she felt like herself again: beautiful.

MEET BOAZ

I KNOW MY REDEEMER LIVES.
(JOB 19:25)

THE WORD "REDEEM' MEANS: to buy back a relative, to be a deliverer, to perform the duty of the near or next kinsfolk, to purchase or ransom.

Ruth lived while the Law of Moses was still in effect, and one of them was the law of redemption, designed to protect people in unfortunate circumstances. The nearest of kin had the right and the responsibility of redeeming his kinsman.

Four things were required for a kinsman to redeem: He must be next of kin (Leviticus 25:25, 25:48; Ruth 3:12–13). He must be able to redeem (Ruth 4:4–6). He must be free of any calamity or need of redemption himself (Ruth 4:6). He must be willing to redeem (Leviticus 25:27; Ruth 4:7–11).

If a family member was forced into slavery, his redeemer purchased his freedom. Likewise, when debt threatened to take away land and livelihood, the kinsman was to step in to redeem the land and let the family live there.

When death came at the hands of another man, the redeemer was to act as the avenger of blood and pursue the killer (Numbers 35:12–34; Deuteronomy 19:1–3). If a family member died without an heir, the kinsman was supposed to marry the widow and rear a son to continue the name of his relative (Genesis 38:8; Deuteronomy 25:5).

If a woman became a widow with no son to provide for her and no daughter to marry off and provide for her, she was left without any income besides what her husband left behind. In most cases, that wasn't much. If there was something to inherit, whichever relative redeemed her took control of her inheritance. The women were at a loss either way. Whether left without anyone to care for them or redeemed by someone who married them out of duty or for their inheritance, it was rare for a man to redeem a widow for love.

If there was no kinsman alive, a woman was stuck waiting for a son to be born into her husband's family who could marry her so the name of the dead could live on. Most young men did not want to marry their brother's widow and give him children before they started their own families.

This left many women hopelessly waiting for what, in most cases, would never come: a second chance at marriage, children, a family of their own, and love. In Ruth's case, Naomi was too old to have more sons after her sons, and her husband died. She had no income or land in

Moab to speak of, so Naomi decided to go back to Bethlehem, be with her own people, and live on her own land, even if she had to live a lowly life.

She told Ruth and Orpah, her daughters-in-law, to go back home to their families, where they might be able to marry someone from their people and start their lives over. Knowing what awaited her as a widow of an Israelite in Bethlehem, Ruth still decided to go with Naomi.

Though Naomi had land in Bethlehem, it was desolate from years of not being tended. Ruth and Naomi's best hope was that one of Naomi's relatives would want the land and redeem them with it. The Bible says, "Now Naomi had a kinsman of her husband's, a man of wealth, of the family of Elimelech, whose name was Boaz" (Ruth 2:1). Boaz was the son of Salmon, who was a descendant of Judah (Matthew 1:5).

Boaz's mother was the woman the Bible refers to as "Rahab the prostitute" (Joshua 6:17). She was the one who hid the Israelite spies when they went into Jericho to spy out the land before going in to possess it. With Rahab as his mother, I'm sure Boaz knew what it was like to be looked down upon because of a questionable background and being different from those around him who was known as God's people. But Rahab did not let her background or what other people thought of her interfere with her faith or stop her from laying hold of her destiny and becoming known as one of God's daughters.

The Bible says of Rahab:

By faith Rahab the prostitute did not perish with those who were disobedient, because she had given a friendly welcome to the spies. (Hebrews 11:31)

Was not Rahab the prostitute justified by works when she received the messengers and sent them out by another way? (James 2:25)

When they got to Bethlehem, Naomi told Ruth to work in Boaz's field to gather enough food for them. It was in his field that Boaz noticed Ruth and was drawn to her. I believe Boaz was drawn to Ruth because her story reminded him so much of his mother's story. He saw in Ruth the same strength of character, faith, and compassion that his mother possessed and passed on to him. He saw her willingness to let go of her past and learn about God. He saw her love for God and her desire to know the true and living God for herself and be one of His people.

Though it is evident that he fell in love with her, Boaz, a man of integrity and honor, treated Ruth as a daughter and showed her much favor. He never approached her with an offer of marriage.

38

At the advice of Naomi, Ruth went to him and pointed out that he could redeem them. However, a nearer relative had the first right of redemption. If Naomi's closer relative would not redeem them and the land, Boaz was prepared to do so.

The man who was nearest of kin agreed to redeem the land until he found out there was a young widow involved, then he refused. That left Boaz, the next of kin, with the right to redeem the land along with Naomi and Ruth.

Boaz met all the criteria for a redeemer. He was the nearest of kin to her deceased husband (Ruth 2:1). He was able to redeem by paying the price of redemption (2:1). He was free from any debt without any need of redemption himself. He was willing to redeem Ruth and Naomi (4:4). Beyond all these things, Boaz loved Ruth and wanted to marry her.

In this same way, God sent Jesus to redeem the human race, cursed and condemned to a life of bondage and sin according to the law. Not only did Jesus meet the criteria, but like Boaz, He redeems us because of His love for us.

However, Jesus paid a much greater price for our redemption than Boaz did for Ruth. "Christ also has loved us and given Himself for us, an offering and a sacrifice to God for a sweet-smelling aroma" (Ephesians 5:2).

> *Not only did Jesus meet the criteria, but like Boaz, He redeems us because of His love for us.*

1) He is our nearest kinsman with authority to redeem us through the incarnation: "Who, being in the form of God, thought it not robbery to be equal with God: but made himself of no reputation, and took upon him the form of a servant, and was made in the likeness of men" (Philippians 2:6-7 KJV).

2) He is able to redeem us: "He is able to save to the uttermost those who draw near to God through Him" (Hebrews 7:25).

3) Christ is free of all calamity and sin: "For we have not a high priest which cannot be touched with the feeling of our infirmities; but was in all points tempted like as we are, yet without sin" (Hebrews 4:15).

4) He is willing to redeem us: "And being found in fashion as a man, he humbled himself, and became obedient unto death, even the death of the cross" (Philippians 2:8 KJV).

Our Redeemer lives, and He is able to save us. It is our responsibility to lie at His feet and say, "Cover me, for you are my Redeemer" (Ruth 3:9).

LOVE

GOD'S LOVE COVERS YOU

HE WILL COVER YOU WITH HIS FEATHERS, AND UNDER HIS WINGS, YOU WILL TAKE REFUGE. (PSALM 91:4 NKJV)

WHEN THE LORD COVERS YOU, He puts a hedge of protection around you, becomes your defender, and brings you into a covenant relationship with Him.

When Boaz was introduced to Ruth in his field, he offered her protection and provision. He also told his men to allow Ruth to glean from his field without harassing her. He told her, *"Now, listen, my daughter, do not go to glean in another field or leave this one, but keep close to my young women" (Ruth 2:8)*. Ruth accepted his offer, and his field became a place of safety for her.

God offers this same provision, and protection Ruth found under Boaz's covering to His daughters who come under His wing. Like a mama bird that covers her little ones with her wings, God hides us in the secret place of His wings where evil cannot find us:

He who dwells in the secret place of the Most High shall abide under the shadow of the Almighty... You shall not be afraid of the terror by night, nor of the arrow that flies by day, nor of the pestilence that walks in darkness, nor of the destruction that lays waste at noonday... Because you have made the Lord, who is my refuge, even the Most High, your dwelling place, no evil shall befall you, nor shall any plague come near your dwelling. (Psalm 91:1, 5-6, 9-10 NKJV)

Though God wants to cover us, it's up to us to come under His covering and stay where He puts us, even when He doesn't reveal His plan. At times, it can be tempting to leave

> **God wants us to abide under His wing for our protection.**

the place of grace where God's provision and protection are because we are drawn to other attractive things.

When we do leave, we become open targets and can easily fall into the devil's snares. The devil knows how to entice us with appealing things, so we, like Eve, might take the bait, only to find out it was a trap all along.

Had Ruth decided to go to another man's field after Boaz warned her not to, she would have stepped out from under his covering and forfeited his protection and provision. She would have been left to face whatever may have come and figure things out on her own. Ruth's obedience brought about her provision and protection, ultimately leading to her marriage to Boaz and her place among God's people.

I've allowed myself to be led astray by the enemy's deception before, and I've watched it happen to other women. It's much harder to get out of a snare than to fall into one. Giving in to temptation is not worth the trouble, heartache, and long-term consequences that follow.

God wants us to abide under His wing for our protection. It's always better to stay where He places us and do what He tells us even when we don't understand His reasons. In everything, seek God in prayer; trust that He knows what's best for you, and wait for His guidance. Beloved, God loves you, and He wants to cover you. Let Him.

GOD LOVES YOU
AS A FATHER

FOR THE LORD DISCIPLINES THE ONE HE LOVES
AND CHASTISES EVERY CHILD WHOM HE RECEIVES.
(HEBREWS 12:6)

THE WORD "CHASTISE" MEANS to instruct, teach, train up a child, or educate and discipline (by punishment if necessary).

Boaz loved Ruth first as a father willing to bring correction and instruction gently and lovingly. One example is when Ruth went to the threshing floor to ask Boaz to redeem her.

She broke protocol. Had people seen her there in the middle of the night, it could have made her look like a woman of impure motives and hindered their chance to marry. Though he did not tell her to leave that night, he had the foresight and love for her to care about how her actions could result in negative consequences.

He instructed her, "'Lie down until the morning.' She lay at his feet until the morning but arose before one could recognize another. And he said, 'Let it not be known that the woman came to the threshing floor' " (Ruth 3:13–14). Thankfully, no one saw Ruth, and all went well.

Boaz was looking out for her best interest, and Ruth obeyed. She stayed at the threshing floor all night, though that probably wasn't her plan, seeing that she had Naomi waiting for her back home.

Just like Boaz, when God tells us to do something, it's because He has our best interest at heart. He knows the protocols and has the foresight to see what consequences our actions might create for us.

The writer of Hebrew exhorts us:

My daughters, do not regard lightly the chastisement of the Lord, nor be weary when reproved by him. It is for chastening that you have to endure. God is treating you as daughters. For what daughter is there whom her father does not chastise? If you are left without chastisement, in which all have participated, then you are illegitimate children and not daughters. (Hebrews 12:5, 7, 8, emphasis added)

Never allow the enemy to make you think God's correction is His rejection. The devil deceived Eve into thinking God was holding something back from her so he could lead her into the snare of disobedience. As a result of her disobedience, she was removed from the Garden of

50

Eden and the presence of God (see Genesis 3). Even though the Lord loved Eve, He disciplined her when she disobeyed Him.

When the Lord trains us for greater things, He corrects us when we miss the mark. He disciplines us when we continue to disobey His instruction.

> **Never allow the enemy to make you think that God's correction is His rejection.**

When we disobey God, and He has to discipline us, it's easy to fall into the trap of blaming Him for the consequences we set in motion. The truth is that God gives us many warnings and many chances to make the corrections He asks of us. He wants us to understand the consequences of disobedience and the blessings of obedience.

Nevertheless, He is not surprised by our disobedience. When we mess up, He has a plan to set us on the right path again. When we repent and renew our obedience to Him, He can make even our mistakes and mess-ups work for our good.

The Lord wants us to learn to obey His first instructions like Ruth did when Boaz instructed her. But when we miss the mark, He wants us to allow Him to correct us immediately. It's better to learn to obey quickly than to endure a long season of chastisement and what can become an open rebuke by Him because of disobedience.

Eve's disobedience created consequences that affected her children and, ultimately, the whole human race. But the Lord had a plan for her deliverance and ours. Her Seed, Jesus Christ, would crush Satan's head under His feet.

When Cain killed Abel, it was partly due to being born into the sinful nature of his parents that was passed down through their disobedience, but the Lord did not hold Eve's sin against her. He gave her another son, Seth, whose name means "substitute" in place of Abel, whom Cain killed (Genesis 4:25).

Eve submitted to God during the time of chastisement. Therefore, He made what the enemy meant to destroy her life, and ours work for her good and ours. God gave her another son as a substitute for the one who sin, and death had claimed. He sent His Son Jesus as a substitute for the human race, whom sin and death had also claimed.

Beloved, the Lord can and will make all things work together for your good if you are willing to endure His chastisement and learn to obey Him.

GOD LOVES
YOU JEALOUSLY

> SET ME AS A SEAL UPON YOUR HEART, AS A SEAL
> UPON YOUR ARM, FOR LOVE IS STRONG AS DEATH,
> JEALOUSY IS FIERCE AS THE GRAVE. ITS FLASHES ARE
> FLASHES OF FIRE, THE VERY FLAME OF THE LORD.
> (SONG OF SOLOMON 8:6)

MOST PEOPLE DON'T LIKE to talk about it, but the Lord is a jealous God—it's one of His names! *Exodus 34:14 says, "You shall worship no other god, for the Lord, whose name is Jealous, is a jealous God."*

In the New Covenant, God's jealousy did not end. Jesus warned the disciples that they would have to be willing to part with even their families if it came down to a choice between their families and God (see Matthew 10:34–39).

> Paul warned the church: "You cannot drink the cup of the Lord and the cup of demons. You cannot partake of the table of the Lord and the table of demons. Shall we provoke the Lord to jealousy? Are we stronger than He?" (1 Corinthians 10:21–22).

Of all the commandments in the Old Covenant, only two made it into the New Covenant: *"Love the Lord your God with all your heart... soul...mind... and love your neighbor as yourself"* (Matthew 22:37–39).

The question that needs to be answered for this generation is: **Why?**

God is jealous because His covenant requires devotion and loyalty.

> *Though the Lord is jealous for you, He will never mistreat you or force you to be in a relationship with Him.*

As any husband would expect of his wife, when we enter into a covenant relationship with Him, God expects us not to commit to anything or anyone that will take us away from our relationship with Him.

When we put other things or people before God, they become our idols. An idol is anything or anyone you give your time and devotion to above and before God.

One of the enemy's ultimate goals is to lure us away from the true and living God by allowing things and people to take His place in our lives, making them the idols we worship. In so doing, we break up our relationship with the Lord. So God commands us to love others but to worship Him only.

Like a loving husband who becomes jealous of a wife being lured away by another man with ill intentions, the Lord's jealousy flares up because He loves us and wants to protect us from the consequences that unfaithfulness brings.

Though the Lord is jealous for you, He will never mistreat you or force you to be in a relationship with Him.

Boaz saw the way other men looked at Ruth. He warned them not to harass her, and he told her to stay in his field where he could watch over her. In his words, *"Have I not charged the young men not to touch you? And when you are thirsty, go to the vessels and drink what the young men have drawn" (Ruth 2:9)*. Boaz desired Ruth well before they married, but he did not force her into a relationship. Boaz was jealous for Ruth, and he wanted to protect her from harm.

Boaz treated Ruth so well that she asked him to marry her. In this same way, God loves us so much He makes us want to commit to Him. *"We love because he first loved us" (1 John 4:19)*.

When Ruth proposed marriage to him, Boaz was surprised that she chose him because of all the younger men she had to choose from (Ruth 3:10). The fidelity Ruth showed Boaz made him love her even more.

Beloved, when you choose God above all else, He demonstrates His love for you by honoring you with His blessing, His favor, and His everlasting covenant.

GOD LOVES
YOU PERFECTLY

WHEN THE PERFECT COMES, THE PARTIAL WILL
PASS AWAY.
(1 CORINTHIANS 13:10)

IN THIS LIFE, OUR ABILITY to understand God's perfect, complete love for us is limited by our perception of reality. His love is unlike our idea of completeness or perfection that can be undone, broken, or changed. God's love cannot and will not change. It is entirely perfect now and forever.

He can never love you more than He does right now. There is nothing you can do or have to do to earn His love or receive more of it. In the same way, you can do nothing to make God love you any less.

On your best day, God doesn't love you anymore; on your worst day, He doesn't love you any less. His love is stable.

Life has a way of clouding our understanding of God's love for us through our circumstances. We all go through things that can sometimes make us question God's love for us and make us feel like He's turned His back on us.

After Naomi's husband and her sons died, she was sure the Lord had turned against her. She feared for her future and eventually gave in to her emotions, which was reflected in the new name she gave herself when she returned to Bethlehem.

> *On your best day, God doesn't love you anymore, and on your worst day, He doesn't love you any less.*

God used Ruth to uncloud Naomi's understanding of His love for her. Ruth helped her see that even in the worst times when life (not God) had dealt her a bitter hand, God's love for her did not change. The love and kindness Ruth showed Naomi helped her recognize the lies her circumstances had caused her to believe.

Because you are His daughter, whenever God's love is put on trial by the issues of life, and it seems He is guilty of not loving you perfectly, He will send someone to help you recognize His perfect love for you. Naomi almost rejected Ruth, the one the Lord sent to her. Later, she was thankful she chose to let Ruth go with her.

Beloved, the truth is: a friend like Ruth may not be sent to you, but what a friend we have in Jesus! He went to the Father so the Holy Spirit could come and dwell inside us.

He is our Comforter, so believe He is with you to lead and guide you into all truth. This truth includes unclouding the Father's love for you (see John 16:4-15).

GOD LOVES YOU THROUGH YOUR FEARS

THERE IS NO FEAR IN LOVE, BUT PERFECT LOVE
CASTS OUT FEAR. FOR FEAR HAS TORMENT, AND
WHOEVER FEARS HAS NOT BEEN PERFECTED IN LOVE.
(1 JOHN 4:18)

RUTH FACED MANY THINGS that would cause any woman's heart to fear – the death of her husband, the uncertainty of her future, the journey to a foreign land, and then being a foreigner in a new land. However, the seed of God's love had been planted in her heart when she made the Lord her God.

In every circumstance Ruth faced, she had to choose to allow her trust in God's love to cast out fear or let her fears rule her emotions and decisions. Ruth decided to trust God and the people He put in her life, Naomi and Boaz. By doing so, she became more mature and understood the depths of God's love for her.

Even though God tells us not to fear, He is patient with us. He knows we tend to be afraid of things we don't understand and cannot control. So he allows us to go through the process of being perfected in love.

> *Every time fear arises and you choose to trust and obey God, you are allowing Him to love you through your fears.*

We grow in our understanding of God's love and come closer to being perfected in love as we realize that God does not scold or become disappointed with us for being afraid. He does not chastise us for giving in to our fears. He waits for us to learn to trust in His love enough to cast off our fears,

Like a woman who has been hurt before and has to learn to trust again, God shows us His love repeatedly until we trust it. Every time fear arises, and you choose to trust and obey God, you are allowing Him to love you through your fears.

Every time fear rears its head, covered in any disguise — family issues, worries, financial troubles, responsibilities, health issues, the fear of death, or whatever may torment you — your faith in God's love can cast out fear.

As we experience God's love shielding us in the face of all fear and walk through the process of being perfected in His love, fear gives way to faith.

Ruth trusted God's perfect love through loss, tragedies, death, and transition. When you face your biggest fears and realize that God's love is enough to get you through and that His love is magnified— not diminished— when you trust Him in your fears, you can say because you know, *"Perfect love casts out fear."*

GOD LOVES
YOU INTO FREEDOM

FOR FREEDOM CHRIST HAS SET US FREE; STAND
FIRM, THEREFORE, AND DO NOT SUBMIT AGAIN TO A
YOKE OF SLAVERY. (GALATIANS 5:1)

ONCE WE HAVE OVERCOME our fears, we are ready to step into the freedom Christ meant for us to live in when He set us free. We are able to become the women God created us to be – women who love, live for Christ, serve others, and have the faith to possess our inheritance.

However, God knew that giving us freedom would present particular challenges, so He equipped us to overcome those challenges. As He loves us through our fears, He loves us into freedom without faultfinding or condemnation. He patiently waits for us to learn how to handle our freedom and discover our boundaries. God gives us boundaries because they help us stay free.

Within your boundaries, your inheritance is attainable. Outside of your boundaries are dangers you may not be aware of. The thing is, your boundaries may not be the same as other people's boundaries. You must learn your boundaries and enjoy your freedom within the boundaries God sets for you. God will let you choose.

> Galatians 3:24-25 says, "The law was our tutor to bring us to Christ, that we might be justified by faith. But after faith has come, we are no longer under a tutor." (NKJV)

When I first became a Christian, I put restrictions on myself. Looking back, they were much like laws. The laws I set for myself tutored my heart, and I learned to live a godly life. I extended my boundaries as I matured in Christ. However, I quickly realized there is a fine line between enjoying our freedom and using our freedom as an opportunity to indulge the flesh. Galatians 5:13 says, "Do not use your freedom as an opportunity for the flesh, but through love, serve one another."

As a Moabitess, Ruth probably practiced pagan customs before she married her first husband, but when she married, she came under the laws of her husband. When her husband died, she could choose whether to serve God or return to her old way of life.

In her decision to continue to serve God, she still had to choose whether to be committed to Him or to serve Him halfheartedly. Ruth left her old ways behind and fully dedicated her life to the

Lord. She decided to live within the boundaries her new life presented to her.

Ruth willingly obeyed Naomi's instructions and the boundaries Boaz set for her to glean only from his field. Because of her obedience, she was free to glean anywhere in his field without fear of trouble.

> *Freedom is enjoying your life within the boundaries you and God agree to without feeling like you're missing out on something.*

Paul warned: "'I have the right to do anything,' you say—but not everything is beneficial. 'I have the right to do anything'—but I will not be mastered by anything" (1 Corinthians 6:12).

You are truly free when you are not in bondage to anything, and you can live contently within the boundaries God sets for you.

True freedom is knowing you can have a drink but choosing not to overindulge. It is knowing you can watch whatever you want but choosing to watch only things pleasing to the Holy Spirit. It's dancing at the party and not feeling guilty.

Freedom is enjoying your life within the boundaries you and God agree to without feeling like you're missing out on something because you've chosen to live a life pleasing to God that now satisfies you.

Ruth was satisfied with the life she chose. She did not feel like she was missing out on anything. She had no regrets about what she had given up or the life she had left behind. Her past experiences only made her value true freedom even more.

Because she was free, Ruth could use her freedom to serve Naomi in love. When you are truly free, God can trust you to use your freedom as an opportunity to serve others.

GOD LOVES YOU INSEPARABLY

FOR I AM SURE THAT NEITHER DEATH NOR LIFE,
NOR ANGELS NOR RULERS, NOR THINGS PRESENT
NOR THINGS TO COME, NOR POWERS, NOR HEIGHT
NOR DEPTH, NOR ANYTHING ELSE IN ALL CREATION,
WILL BE ABLE TO SEPARATE US FROM THE LOVE OF
GOD IN CHRIST JESUS OUR LORD.
(ROMANS 8:38–39)

THE WORD "INSEPARABLE" means no space in between and impossible to break apart. Ruth loved her mother-in-law so much that she was willing to walk by faith into the unforeseen future, not knowing what to expect, good or bad. When Naomi started her journey back to Bethlehem, she told both of her daughters-in-law to go back, but Ruth refused and took an oath:

> Do not urge me to leave you or to return from following you. For where you go I will go, and where you lodge I will lodge. Your people shall be my people, and your God my God. Where you die I will die, and there will I be buried. May the Lord do so to me and more also if anything but death separates me from you. (Ruth 1:16–17, emphasis added)

Ruth vowed by the Lord's name to let nothing but death separate her from her mother-in-law, and the two became inseparable from that point on.

> *You can reject God's love, but no one has the power or authority to separate you from God's love.*

As much as Ruth loved Naomi, God loves you more. There is nothing in all creation that can separate you from His love. Just as it is impossible for God to lie, He has promised and made it impossible to separate His love from us.

This present world and all its suffering cannot separate you from the love of God. The devil, try as he might, to accuse us day and night before the Lord, with hopes that God will somehow find us guilty as charged and take His love back, will forever fail.

God has already made up His mind. He already went through the worst we can do and declared when He gave His Son that nothing would be able to separate us from His love.

It is simply impossible for all of eternity for God's love to part from you. You can reject God's love, but no one has the power or authority to separate you from God's love.

Naomi almost made the mistake of rejecting Ruth's love. But, *"When she saw that she was determined to go with her, she stopped speaking to her... and the two of them went until they came to Bethlehem"* (Ruth 1:18-19).

Just as Naomi was tested, you will be too. It's up to you to abide in God's love when life's troubles try to separate you.

GOD LOVE YOU
UNFAILINGLY

LOVE NEVER FAILS.
(1 CORINTHIANS 13:8)

GOD'S LOVE NEVER WEAKENS or stops working. People can confess their unfailing love and allegiance to you and still walk away when love becomes difficult to sustain. This kind of love is what the Bible describes as the mental, emotional love philía—a love that friends share. It can and does fail with time and circumstances. Friends leave us and take their love with them.

However, the unfailing agape love of God is love out of a sense of moral responsibility to love your neighbor as you would yourself, to ensure their safety and wellbeing as you would your own—until the end.

Jesus is a friend that sticks closer than family. He never leaves or forsakes us (Proverbs 18:24; Hebrews 13:5).

Love's commitment is this: to stay lit through all of life's seasons like an ember that refuses to burn out. In the good times, God's love is like the flicker burning atop a sweet-scented candle; it fills the atmosphere and brings comfort and rest.

> *Love's commitment is this: to stay lit through all of life's seasons.*

In the hard times, God's love is like the fire that led the children of Israel through the wilderness; fierce and sure, a shield of protection amid danger.

Ruth's love for Naomi proved to be the agape kind. Ruth's love stayed constant and reliable through the different seasons of Naomi's life. This unfailing love caused Naomi to finally rest because she knew Ruth wouldn't leave her and would always look after her best interest.

God rewarded Ruth beyond her highest imagination for loving Naomi unfailingly; through her fears and into freedom, from brokenness and bitterness to being pleasant and joyful again.

Those who came to know them had this to say about Ruth: *"Your daughter-in-law, who loves you, is more to you than seven sons"* (Ruth 4:15).

You can't give what you don't have. Ruth could love Naomi unfailingly because she had laid hold of God's unfailing love for her. God also wants you to receive His unfailing love for you.

Then and only then can you show His unfailing love to others.

GOD'S LOVE YOU EVERLASTINGLY

I HAVE LOVED YOU WITH AN EVERLASTING LOVE;
THEREFORE, WITH LOVING-KINDNESS HAVE DRAWN
YOU. (JEREMIAH 31:3)

THE LORD DREW RUTH into a relationship with Him and Naomi back into a close relationship with Him through His loving kindness. It was because of His everlasting love for them that He led Boaz to redeem them.

He gave Ruth a son to ensure the legacy of His love for Naomi and Ruth was carried forward beyond their generation. When Boaz and Ruth's son was born, the women of the village came to Naomi and said of the child,

"Blessed be the Lord, who has not left you this day without a redeemer, and may his name be renowned in Israel! He shall be to you a restorer of life and a nourisher of your old age" (Ruth 4:14–15).

The child was named Obed, which means worshipper. Obed was the grandfather of King David, with whom the Lord made an everlasting covenant.

> **God is committed to His covenant of everlasting love with you.**

It is the same covenant the Lord desires to make with all His children, established on His Son, Jesus Christ, the ultimate gift of love:

> Incline your ear, and come to me; hear, that your soul may live; and I will make with you an everlasting covenant, my steadfast, sure love for David. *(Isaiah 55:2–3)*

Like his grandfather Obed, David was a worship like so much so that in David, the Lord said He *"found a man after His own heart"* (1 Samuel 13:14).

God swore to David that one of his sons would always be seated on the throne of Israel because of his heart for the Lord (see Isaiah 9:7 and Luke 1:32). The Lord kept His word to David and, in doing so, showed His eternal love to Ruth. Kings from David's lineage ruled every generation until Jesus, the Eternal King, the "son of David," sat on His heavenly throne (Matthew 1:1). Every time Jesus' genealogy is read, Obed's name is included as the son of Boaz and Ruth.

God has continually kept His everlasting covenant of love with Ruth through her grandson David, and God is committed to His covenant of eternal love with you. He wants to create a legacy of love with you so that your children and your children's children can benefit from God's covenant with you throughout eternity.

Beloved, it's up to you to lay hold of God's love and enter into His everlasting covenant so He can establish you and your generations for all eternity.

QUESTIONS

1. What are the conditions to be a redeemer?
2. How did Jesus meet the conditions to be the Redeemer of the whole world?
3. What has Jesus redeemed you from?
4. What does it mean to come under God's covering?
5. What is one thing God wants you to understand when He disciplines you?
6. What does God require of those who enter into a relationship with Him?
7. What makes God jealous?
8. Can you think of a time when God loved you through your fears?
9. How did He express His love to you during that time?
10. How has God's love led you into freedom in one or more areas of your life?
11. Have you ever felt separated from God's love?
12. If so, how did you get past the feeling and reconnect with the love of God?

13. How has God proved His unfailing love for you?

14. How are you building a legacy of God's everlasting love for your coming generations?

PRAYER

Father, thank you for being such a good Father and loving me so much that you gave your Son to redeem me. Thank you that your love covers me. Please help me to stay under the covering of your wings where your protection and provision are given freely.

When you need to chastise me, help me not to mistake discipline for rejection, and help me to understand that you are jealous for me because of your love for me.

Help me to run to you, not away from you, when I am afraid. Thank you for loving me through my fears and into freedom. Help me to remember each day that you love me unfailingly, inseparably, and everlastingly, and to step fully into your love. Finally, Father, I thank you for the legacy of love that is being built up for my future generations; in Jesus' name, Amen.

ACCEPTANCE

YOU ARE ACCEPTED
IN THE BELOVED

HAVING PREDESTINED US TO ADOPTION AS
[DAUGHTERS] BY JESUS CHRIST TO HIMSELF, AC-
CORDING TO THE GOOD PLEASURE OF HIS WILL, TO
THE PRAISE OF THE GLORY OF HIS GRACE, BY WHICH
HE MADE US ACCEPTED IN THE BELOVED.
(EPHESIANS 1:5-6 EMPHASIS ADDED)

ACCEPTANCE IS MORE THAN being admitted
into a clique or a club. Acceptance is being spe-
cially chosen in love without pretense and having
grace, honor, and abundant favor bestowed
upon you by the One who chose you.

It is no coincidence that Paul chose to use the
same Greek word "charitoo" to tell believers that
we are *accepted in the Beloved*" (Ephesians
1:6), as the angel Gabriel used when he called
Mary "highly favored" in Luke's account of their
exchange: *"And having come in, the angel said
to her, 'Rejoice, highly favored one, the Lord is
with you; blessed are you among women!' "*
(Luke 1:26–28).

The word "charitoo" means to have grace. To
be clothed with special honor, to make accepted, and to be highly favored. When Paul

said we are *"accepted in the Beloved,"* he was saying that in Christ, we have been granted the same favor God showed Mary when He chose her in love to bring forth the Messiah.

Mary was no different from any other young Jewish woman. She said of herself, *"The Lord has looked upon the lowly" (Luke 1:48).* The Lord chose Mary not because she was better than anyone else but out of the council and delight of His own will. That is the same reason He chose Ruth and the same reason He chose you and me.

Faith is God's only requirement to receive His acceptance and every blessing that comes along with it (Hebrews 11:6). Mary responded in faith to God's favor.

> *Luke 1:45 says, "Blessed is she who believed, for there will be a fulfillment of those things which were told her from the Lord."*

I'm sure some people never accepted Mary or believed her story. I'm sure some chose to believe that our Savior was the product of an ill-begotten pregnancy.

I don't think what other people thought of her mattered to Mary. It did not matter if they accepted her or believed her story. Mary believed what the Lord had spoken to her,

> **Faith is God's only requirement to receive His acceptance.**

and she was able to rest in His grace and favor and experience His plan for her life come to pass.

Ruth was a Moabitess woman among the children of Israel. I can imagine that not everyone accepted her right away. However, she did not allow other people's opinions of her to keep her from living in God's acceptance. Besides God, Naomi and Boaz's acceptance of her was all that truly mattered.

Even though God accepts you, some people will try to make you feel like you don't belong where He placed you. People may look down upon you because of your past, their assumptions about you, or simply because you are different from them. But if God is for you and accepts you, His favor and grace will lead you into the place and the inheritance He has for you.

Sadly, we often value people's acceptance above God's acceptance. As a result, we stay in relationships and situations that are not right for us in search of acceptance. We go into new relationships and opportunities without seeking God in prayer to direct us into His favor in search of acceptance. God wants us to seek acceptance in Him and learn to accept ourselves so we won't settle for the wrong kind of acceptance and forfeit our inheritance in Him.

When Naomi and Ruth arrived in Bethlehem, Ruth asked Naomi, *"Please let me go to the field, and glean heads of grain after him in whose sight*

I may find favor" (Ruth 2:2). Ruth could have tried to glean from any field, but by wisdom, she chose to go in the way of God's favor.

When you choose to receive the gift of God's acceptance, He will set people along your path who will accept you, favor you, and help you step into your destiny.

YOU ARE ACCEPTED BECAUSE OF NOT IN SPITE OF WHO YOU ARE

HE CHOSE US IN HIM BEFORE THE FOUNDATION OF
THE WORLD, THAT WE SHOULD BE HOLY AND WITH-
OUT BLAME BEFORE HIM IN LOVE.
(EPHESIANS 1:4)

BOAZ WAS DRAWN TO RUTH because of who she was, not in spite of who she was. He knew about her past and their cultural differences, but he did not let those things distract him from getting to know Ruth's heart. He looked at the covenant she entered with her mother-in-law and the Lord. He saw her as God saw her: a beautiful Moabite woman worthy of love and acceptance.

When Ruth asked Boaz why he favored her, he answered her with these words:

It has been fully reported to me, all that you have done for your mother-in-law since the death of your husband, and how you have left your father and your mother and the land of your birth, and have come to a people whom you did not know before. The Lord repay your work, and a full reward be given

*you by the Lord God of Israel, under whose
wings you have come for refuge. (Ruth 2:10–
12)*

When Boaz looked at
Ruth, he saw a woman with
a heart for God. Boaz rec-
ognized that God knew she
was a Moabite and had
accepted and favored
Ruth.

> **The Lord uses
> all your expe-
> riences to
> mold you into
> the woman He
> created you
> to be.**

God did not hold Ruth's
cultural and racial back-
ground against her. Nor did He hold the idolatry
of her past against her. The Lord saw a heart willing to leave behind all she had and knew to follow Him and care for her mother-in-law.

God looks at you in this same way. He knows
your history and your cultural background. He
knows your worldly traditions and your weak-
nesses. He knows the things you are going
through right now. He chose you before you were
born. He loved you and accepted you before
you ever knew Him. Not in spite of who you are
but because of who you are in Him.

When people reject you, don't hold it against
them. Know that God has people who will accept and receive you as a blessing. The Lord uses
all of your experiences to mold you into the
woman He created you to be so that you can be
a witness to other women in your generation. So

others can relate to you and feel at ease being transparent with you, and you can have compassion on them because you can relate to them. So you can lead others standing where you've been — out of darkness and into God's light.

Don't be ashamed of your past, who you are, or what you're going through. Be confident in who God created you to be. Other women need you to be.

YOU ARE ACCEPTED WITHOUT PRETENSE

O LORD, YOU HAVE SEARCHED ME AND KNOWN
ME! YOU KNOW WHEN I SIT DOWN AND WHEN I RISE
UP, YOU DISCERN MY THOUGHTS FROM AFAR. YOU
SEARCH OUT MY PATH AND MY LYING DOWN AND ARE
ACQUAINTED WITH ALL MY WAYS.
(PSALM 139:1–3)

YOU DON'T HAVE TO PRETEND to be someone you are not with God. He wants you to have an authentic relationship with Him, knowing that He sees the real you — your thoughts and the intentions of your heart — and loves and accepts you.

When Naomi advised Ruth to go to Boaz about redeeming them, she gave her some instructions according to the protocol of her people:

> Therefore wash yourself and anoint yourself, put on your best garment and go down to the threshing floor; but do not make yourself known to the man until he has finished eating and drinking. (Ruth 3:3, emphasis added)

In not making herself known, Ruth was waiting for the right time to approach Boaz. This was not a form of deception, as pretense often is. She was not afraid for him to find out who she was; she used protocol to approach him. When Boaz asked who was at his feet, Ruth identified herself and said, *"I am Ruth, your maidservant"* (Ruth 3:8).

We enter into a relationship with the Lord by grace through faith. We enter into His presence by the blood of the Lamb. We are cleansed by the washing of the water of His word and anointed with the oil of His Spirit. Like Ruth when she went to Boaz, we are to come before the Lord cleansed, anointed, covered, and willing to wait upon Him as ourselves, not pretending to be who or what we are not.

When I first became a Christian and joined my church, I had no idea what organized religion was like or what was expected of me. I was passionate but did not understand God's protocols. After being in church for some time, I was called into ministry. As I started to take on more of a role in the church, I tried to be like other women in ministry.

One day the Lord spoke to me with a still, small voice and said,

> *"I desire an authentic relationship with you. Do not come into my presence with pre-*

*tense. You cannot build an authentic rela-
tionship with me unless you come to me genuinely. Do not try to change who you are. I
knew who you were when I called you."*

Those words changed
my life and my perspective
of God. It wasn't that God
did not expect me to grow
into a mature Christian or
take off my old ways. He
wanted me to be the new
creation He created me to
be, but genuinely as myself.

> **You don't
> have to pre-
> tend to be
> someone you
> are not with
> God.**

*Hebrews 13:7 says, "Remember your leaders,
those who spoke to you the word of God.
Consider the outcome of their way of life
and imitate their faith."*

We are supposed to imitate the faith of those
who lead us and have obtained the promises of
God. However, this does not mean we should try
to be just like them in their lives and personalities.
If God wanted everyone to be, look, and sound
alike, He could have easily created us that way.
But He chose instead to make each one of us as
unique as our fingerprints.

Romans 12:4-5 says:

*For as in one body, we have many members,
and the members do not all have the same
function, so we, though many, are one body*

*in Christ, and individually members one of
another.*

When I realized I did not have to be like other
women and that God did not want me to, I
gained the freedom to grow into the authentic
representation of Christ as the woman God created me to be.

The foundation of every good and lasting relationship is authenticity. Knowing that I could be
myself allowed me to grow a relationship with the
God who sees me, knows me, and wants a relationship with me. Not the perfect representation
of who I thought He wanted me to be.

Boaz accepted Ruth as a Moabitess who
made the Lord her God and His people her people. Ruth became God's daughter by faith because she imitated the faith she saw in her
mother-in-law and let God change her heart.
Similarly, God doesn't want you to pretend to be
someone else for Him. He accepts you just as you
are.

God is a gentleman. He waits for us to come
to Him and make ourselves known. Then He re-
veals the things that need to be removed that
would hinder us from growing into the godly
women He created us to be.

YOU ARE WORKS
ARE ACCEPTED

FOR WE ARE HIS WORKMANSHIP, CREATED IN
CHRIST JESUS FOR GOOD WORKS, WHICH GOD PRE-
PARED BEFOREHAND, THAT WE SHOULD WALK IN
THEM. (EPHESIANS 2:10)

WE ARE ALL CALLED TO do different works in different seasons, but as God's daughters, everything we do should be a part of the good works God planned for us.

Your work may be to raise your family, start a ministry, have a career, or do all these things simultaneously or in different seasons. These are all good. As long as you do what God calls you to do in the season He calls you to do it and do it with all your heart, he accepts your works.

When Ruth's husband died, one season ended, and another season of life began. She was faced with the choice of staying in Moab, where things might have been easier, or going to Bethlehem to take care of her mother-in-law, where things would be much harder for her.

Ruth chose to go to Bethlehem, where she would have to work to provide for herself and Naomi. She accepted the season and did the work necessary to make it through that time in their lives.

We all go through different seasons in life, and often the works God calls us to can and do change with our seasons. Change can make us feel uncomfortable and confused. It could be returning to work after having a child, staying home with children after working outside the home or taking a lesser-paying job. It could be taking on more responsibility for your job, starting a business, or caring for a loved one. Changes can be challenging to get through if we don't see all of our work as part of the good we are called to do.

God wants us to look at work from His perspective. He wants us to serve others and be content in whatever we do.

Colossians 3:23–24 says:

Don't look for your reward from others. Whatever you do, work heartily, as for the Lord and not for men, knowing that from the Lord you will receive the inheritance as your reward. You are serving the Lord Christ.

Ruth worked hard with a pure heart and pure motives at a lowly job to provide for her family. She did not let her job define her or take away her self-worth. God can and will bless us while doing the work we think is mediocre when we are faithful to our calling in each season of our lives.

> **Often the works God calls us to can and do change with our seasons.**

Ruth's decision to serve her mother-in-law and work willingly with her hands to support Naomi was a good work and acceptable to God (Proverbs 31:13).

Because her motives were pure, God honored Ruth's good works and led her into His perfect plan. Boaz realized that Ruth could have chosen a different life, which made him admire her even more. Boaz's decision to marry Ruth and give her a better life was partly influenced by her good works.

When we work for material rewards and worldly success, we don't always get back what we put in, which can leave us feeling disappointed.

However, God accepts and rewards the work we put into our marriages, raising our families, doing our jobs, growing our businesses, building a ministry, or anything else when we do it as servants with a good attitude and sincere hearts. Don't allow the world or people who don't understand how God is leading you to define what success should look like for you.

Every season, success is defined the same way – knowing and doing God's will. This Beloved is how you will receive your reward.

YOUR PRAYERS
ARE ACCEPTED

BUT AS FOR ME, MY PRAYER IS TO YOU, O LORD,
IN THE ACCEPTABLE TIME; O GOD, IN THE MULTITUDE
OF YOUR MERCY, HEAR ME IN THE TRUTH OF YOUR
SALVATION. (PSALM 69:13)

FOR THOSE OF US who have received Jesus as our Savior, our acceptable time is now. The Lord hears our prayers spoken according to His will and wants us to have confidence that He answers them.

1 John 5:14-15 says:

Now this is the confidence that we have in Him, that if we ask anything according to His will, He hears us. And if we know that He hears us, whatever we ask, we know that we have the petitions that we have asked of Him.

We won't always get the answers in the way and time we hope for them, but we can be sure that God will answer us.

Naomi had no hope for a better future for herself in Moab or Bethlehem, but she still had enough confidence in God to pray for her daughters-in-law. Before Naomi began her journey back home, she put her prayers and petitions before the Lord:

> Naomi said to her two daughters-in-law, "Go, return each of you to her mother's house. May the Lord deal kindly with you, as you have dealt with the dead and with me. The Lord grant that you may find rest, each of you in the house of her husband!" Then she kissed them, and they lifted up their voices and wept. (Ruth 1:8–9)

I assume that Ruth must have watched Naomi pray and put her trust in God many times before that day, throughout the different seasons of their life together when Naomi lived as a widow and when her sons passed away.

Ruth's confidence in God must have been built up every time she watched Naomi pray and saw God answer. Even when her prayers weren't answered as she had hoped each time, she still witnessed a loving God's mercy, compassion, and attentiveness.

Why else would Ruth declare, "Your God will be my God" (Ruth 1:16) after witnessing all the suffering Naomi went through?

was there a model in your life?

Is your life and responses to life's difficulties & joys a model to build up another's confidence in God?

104

I can imagine that Ruth took every one of Naomi's prayers to heart, and that day was no different. Only that day Ruth put her own confidence and trust in God, and God used Ruth to answer Naomi's prayer

> **You don't have to know the perfect will of God to pray the will of God.**

above what she could ask for or imagine.

Naomi prayed that the Lord would show kindness to Orpah and Ruth. She prayed that He would give them new husbands and that they would find rest with their husbands.

Naomi did not know how God would do it, but she knew that a loving God would want these young women to have husbands, another chance at love, a family, and children.

She knew it wasn't God's will to punish them for their husbands' sins or mistakes. Naomi prayed according to what she knew about God's mercy and His will. She left the rest to Him, as I'm sure she'd done many times before.

You don't have to know the perfect will of God to pray the will of God. You only need to pray according to the truth you find in His word, what you know of His character, and what has been revealed to you by His Spirit. Then put your confidence in God, knowing He accepts your prayers and will answer them.

The Lord answered Naomi's prayers for Ruth through Boaz. When Naomi saw that Boaz favored Ruth, she realized the Lord was answering her prayers in His way and His own time, above what she asked for:

> And her mother-in-law said to her, "Where have you gleaned today? And where did you work? Blessed be the one who took notice of you." So she told her mother-in-law with whom she had worked, and said, "The man's name with whom I worked today is Boaz." Then Naomi said to her daughter-in-law, "Blessed be he of the Lord, who has not forsaken His kindness to the living and the dead!" (Ruth 2:19-20)

The Lord blessed Naomi through her prayer for Ruth, who continued caring for her mother-in-law after she married Boaz.

The Lord wants to answer your prayers. However, those answers require you to trust God even when you cannot understand Him. Like Naomi, you will need to open the eyes of your understanding to see the Lord working out the answers to your prayers according to His counsel.

YOUR SACRIFICE
IS ACCEPTED

YOU COME TO HIM, A LIVING STONE REJECTED BY
MEN, BUT IN THE SIGHT OF GOD CHOSEN AND PRE-
CIOUS, YOU YOURSELVES LIKE LIVING STONES ARE BE-
ING BUILT UP AS A SPIRITUAL HOUSE, TO BE A HOLY
PRIESTHOOD, TO OFFER SPIRITUAL SACRIFICES AC-
CEPTABLE TO GOD THROUGH JESUS CHRIST.
(1 PETER 2:4-5)

TO OFFER A SACRIFICE is to willingly give something up or to lay down one's life in place of another so the other can live.

Christ has already been sacrificed once and
for all. We never have to offer sacrifice for our sins
again. However, the Lord asks us to be living
stones and offer spiritual sacrifices, to die to the
flesh so His Spirit can live through us. It takes a life
of sacrifice to live by the Spirit.

The Spirit of life and the flesh (human nature
without God) are constantly at war in every born-
again believer.

Galatians 5:16-17 says:

*Walk by the Spirit, and you will not gratify the
desires of the flesh. For the desires of the flesh*

are against the Spirit, and the desires of the Spirit are against the flesh, for these are opposed to each other, to keep you from doing the things you want to do.

Naomi tried to talk her out of it, but Ruth still gave up her future in Moab to go into an unknown future with her mother-in-law. Ruth's decision went against the nature of the flesh, which desires to please itself first.

When we read about Ruth's life, written like a beautiful love story, it's easy to overlook that she by no means had an easy life when she first arrived in Bethlehem. Ruth knew it would not be easy, but with a yielded and determined heart, she decided to follow Naomi no matter what. She said, *"Where you die I will die, and there I will be buried" (Ruth 1:17).* This was a spiritual sacrifice acceptable to the Lord.

Ruth found favor with Boaz, and he told the men who worked for him to treat her with respect. Yet, I'm sure some women and men did not think so kindly of her. After all, she was a Moabite, and Boaz favored her over the other women

> **When we choose to do things God's way over our way, we offer spiritual sacrifice.**

working in his field before Ruth got there. Why else would he have to make sure they all treated her well? Besides that, gleaning barley was no walk in the park. But Ruth set her mind on the things of God, yielded herself to Him, and did things His way.

Like Ruth, we offer a spiritual sacrifice when we choose to do things God's way over our way. Every time we obey the voice of the Holy Spirit, we offer the Lord a spiritual sacrifice.

Every time you choose gentleness, quietness, and kindness against the will of the flesh, you offer a precious and costly sacrifice pleasing to the Lord (see 1 Peter 3:4). Every time you put someone else's needs above your own, you offer a spiritual sacrifice. You offer a spiritual sacrifice when you give up your comfort to help someone. Every time you praise God instead of complaining, bless those who curse you, and pray for those who despitefully use and abuse you, you offer God spiritual sacrifice.

Beloved, these are the sacrifices God desires from each one of us. They will never be rejected or turned away.

Which fruit of the spirit comes easiest to you? Hardest?

Galatians 5:22-23

YOUR SUFFERING IS ACCEPTED

WHEN YOU DO GOOD AND SUFFER FOR IT, YOU ENDURE, THIS IS ACCEPTABLE IN THE SIGHT OF GOD. FOR TO THIS, YOU HAVE BEEN CALLED, BECAUSE CHRIST ALSO SUFFERED FOR YOU, LEAVING YOU AN EXAMPLE, SO THAT YOU MIGHT FOLLOW IN HIS STEPS. (1 PETER 2:20-21)

SUFFERING AND SACRIFICE ARE not the same. You can suffer without sacrifice, but you cannot sacrifice without suffering to some degree.

It is not a sacrifice when we suffer for doing the wrong thing. It is the consequences of our actions. However, when we suffer for doing good and maintaining a humble spirit, it becomes a well-pleasing sacrifice that is holy and acceptable to God.

Ruth sacrificed her life to do well by her mother-in-law, putting Naomi's needs above her own, and with her sacrifice came suffering. Ruth went to Bethlehem with Naomi, knowing that they both might be destined to a life of suffering if a redeemer did not provide protection and provision.

Ruth and Naomi journeyed from Moab to Bethlehem as two women alone. Since Naomi was the older woman, it is safe to assume that Ruth carried the greatest load of the trip. When they got to Bethlehem, Ruth went out to find work in Boaz's field by herself.

I'm sure this brought Ruth a level of mental and emotional suffering. Her body also endured physical suffering because she worked in the fields all day. Ruth did not complain about her work or her circumstance. She was thankful for the opportunity to provide for her mother-in-law and herself. God saw her suffering with a good attitude and rewarded her.

Don't ever think that God doesn't see your suffering. God promises that when we suffer like Christ, we will reign with Christ (see Timothy 2:12). An attitude of humility when you suffer for the sake of doing good is what allows God's strength to be manifested in your weakness, and it prepares you for promotion.

Ruth did not know it, but she was being prepared for promotion. Boaz took notice of what Ruth was doing for her mother-in-law, and he favored her. She went from working in the field to owning it with her husband.

Beloved, God wants you to know that anytime He allows you to suffer for the sake of doing good, He is preparing you for promotion. He makes all things—even our suffering—work together for our good if we love God and are called according to His purpose (Romans 8:28). If you have been suffering for doing good and have endured in the manner Christ endured, be encouraged. Know that promotion is on the way.

— what does suffering with a good attitude look like to you?

QUESTIONS

1. What does it mean to be accepted by God?
2. Why does God accept us for who we are?
3. What makes our works acceptable to God?
4. Who do Christians ultimately work for?
5. How can you be content in whatever season you're in?
6. How do you define success?
7. How can you pray for the will of God if you don't have specific information?
8. Have you ever experienced God answering your prayer in an unexpected way?
9. What is a spiritual sacrifice?
10. Why does God ask for spiritual sacrifices?
11. What is your most significant spiritual sacrifice?
12. What kind of attitude should we have when we suffer?
13. How does God use suffering to prepare us for promotion?

PRAYER

Father, I thank you that I am accepted in the Beloved. Help me to step fully into the embrace of your acceptance so I can experience the full measure of your favor. Thank You, Father, that I am accepted because of, not in spite of, who I am.

When I'm in doubt, help me remember that you accept my works, prayers, sacrifice, and suffering when I do that onto you, and help me keep a good and pleasant attitude. Give me the courage and the confidence to accept myself and be all you called me to be. In Jesus' name, Amen.

BEAUTY

YOU ARE ALTOGETHER BEAUTIFUL

YOU ARE ALTOGETHER BEAUTIFUL, MY LOVE;
THERE IS NO FLAW IN YOU.
(SONG OF SOLOMON 4:7)

GOD CREATED WOMEN altogether beautiful–
on the inside and the outside. He formed us with
the seed of His beauty in our hearts so that we
can reflect His beauty.

He perfectly knit each of us together– body,
features, and hue, to fit our individual and unique
identities. He also put a distinct purpose in us
when we were made so that we can each display His beauty in our own way.

God desires us, who are His daughters, to embrace ourselves and believe that we are altogether beautiful.

TWO KINDS OF BEAUTY

How beautiful and pleasant you are, O
loved one, with all your delights!
(Song of Solomon 7:6)

Most women would agree that beauty is
more than our makeup, hair, clothes, and body
type. Most women would also agree that authentic beauty is primarily defined by our character
and what's in our hearts. Even though most believe real beauty begins in the heart, most
women still focus on their outward appearance
more than their hearts.

God wants us to understand that there are
two kinds of beauty. We shouldn't neglect either,
but the beauty of the heart should be our primary
focus. Outward beauty should be secondary.
Making outer beauty our main focus makes us
vain. That is what happened to Tyre. After God
created him with beauty and arrayed him in the
most beautiful jewels in all creation, he became
prideful because of all his splendor, and in vain,
he rebelled against God (Ezekiel 27).

Vain beauty is the opposite of the beauty women who fear the Lord possesses (Proverbs 31:30). Vain beauty grows in the hearts of women who focus on their outward appearance and don't have submitted hearts towards the Lord.

> *It is up to you to embrace the outward beauty God created you with and to nurture your inward beauty.*

The Lord plants His beauty in each one of His daughters' hearts. The Lord's beauty is referred to as "na'om" in Hebrew. It has the same root word used in Naomi's name, which means pleasant. The full meaning is agreeableness, splendor, kindness, delightfulness, perfection, majesty, grace, and pleasantness. This beauty is spiritual, just as God is a Spirit.

King David said:

One thing have I desired of the Lord and that one thing will I seek, that I may dwell in the house of the Lord all the days of my life to behold the beauty of the Lord, and to inquire in His temple. (Psalm 27:4)

When we walk closely with the Holy Spirit, our communion becomes so intimate that we can get caught up in His presence's kindness, delightfulness, perfection, majesty, grace, and pleasantness. This closeness is to behold His beauty.

The two-fold beauty God wants all women to experience is both physical and spiritual. Esther had this kind of beauty, and so did Ruth. When the Bible describes Esther's beauty, two words are used: *tob,* which means to be gracious, pleasant, and of a merry heart, and mar-eh', which means to be attractive, good-looking, fair, and pleasurable to look upon (Esther 2:7). Esther was beautiful on the inside and the outside.

Though all women were created with the potential to develop this kind of two-fold beauty, not all women will. Inner beauty is more costly than the most expensive makeup and clothes we can buy. We can put on pretty, but we must work at cultivating spiritual fruit to develop inner beauty.

Like Ruth and Naomi, godly beauty flourishes in us when we choose to have a pleasant and gentle attitude, learn to be a delight to those around us, and show kindness and graciousness to all people. It diminishes when we choose the opposite attitudes.

Beloved, you were created altogether beautiful, without flaw. It is up to you to embrace the outward beauty God created you with and to nurture your inward beauty as God's daughter.

YOU ARE INCORRUPTIBLY BEAUTIFUL

DO NOT LET YOUR ADORNMENT BE MERELY OUT-
WARD—ARRANGING THE HAIR, WEARING GOLD, OR
PUTTING ON FINE APPAREL—RATHER LET IT BE THE
HIDDEN PERSON OF THE HEART, WITH THE INCOR-
RUPTIBLE BEAUTY OF A GENTLE AND QUIET SPIRIT,
WHICH IS VERY PRECIOUS IN THE SIGHT OF GOD.
(1 PETER 3:3-4)

INCORRUPTIBLE EVERLASTING BEAUTY is the seed of God's image, planted in the heart of every one of God's daughters. Despite any external conditions, it will grow in the heart of good soil if you water it.

The Bible defines the heart as the thoughts and feelings of a person. The mind or middle of a person. The part of our being that is connected to God and our world experiences. It is the seat of our emotions, our innermost secret place.

With the heart, we love, we hate, we covet, we crave, we forgive, we re- member, and we forget. Salvation happens when we believe in our hearts. Doubt and unforgiveness also occur in our hearts.

> **We either nurture beauty or bitterness.**

All our experiences—good or bad—are felt and processed in our hearts. What we let stay and what we let go determines the quality of our soil. We either nurture beauty or bitterness.

Like Ruth and Naomi, most women have ex- perienced at least one unpleasant, painful event in life. Many have experienced worse things than Naomi and Ruth, including loss, rejection, be- trayal, being taken advantage of, molestation, rape, abuse, miscarriage, or abortion.

The way we process painful experiences de- termines what grows in our hearts. Bitterness, pride, bondage, fear, or feelings of unworthiness left unchecked can turn into bitterness. Allowing jealousy, distrust, manipulation, anger, resent- ment, and unforgiveness to linger can also cause bitterness to grow.

When bitterness grows, it affects us and those we influence (see Hebrews 12:15). Naomi had a significant influence over Ruth. If she had allowed the bitterness in her heart to grow, she would have contaminated Ruth's faith (Hebrews 12:15) and ruined any chances for their redemption.

> **When bitterness grows, it affects us as well as those we have influence over.**

However, Naomi put her feelings aside, let go of the bitterness, and reclaimed her pleasant attitude. By doing this, she encouraged Ruth's faith.

After a while, Naomi's pleasant attitude wasn't just about encouraging Ruth; hope began to spring up in her heart, and her beauty began to bloom again.

We will all experience feelings that can produce bitterness at some point. But if we want godly beauty, we will have to learn, like Naomi did, to let things go and respond to life's unpleasant events with a pleasant attitude, so the soil of our hearts will be a place where the godly kind of beauty can grow.

Ephesians 5:1-2 says, "Therefore be imitators of God, as beloved children." God is gentle and quiet, pleasant and kind. We demonstrate His gentleness when we have compassionate and humble attitudes.

Quietness, translated as *"to be still,"* means to rest in God and have undisturbed inner peace. This quietness is demonstrated best when things disturb our peace, but our hearts remain fixed and stable, trusting that God can guide us through any unsettling trial (see Psalm 112:8).

I believe Ruth grew in her understanding of godly beauty as she repeatedly watched Naomi demonstrate God's gentleness, quietness, and pleasantness. Because of Naomi's example, Ruth was able to develop spiritual beauty and demonstrate this same gentleness and kindness throughout her own experiences.

The beauty of Ruth's gentle spirit brought her the reward of a caring and loving husband in Boaz. He saw the reflection of the beautiful One in her.

When Boaz and Ruth discussed the reasons he showed her favor, he did not mention her outward appearance. He called her virtuous (see Ruth 3:11). Whatever Ruth's appearance, Boaz seemed more taken with her character.

Ruth's gentleness earned her respect, honor, and a place among those new people in a new land. *David said of the Lord, "You have given me the shield of your salvation, and your right hand supported me, and your gentleness made me great" (Psalm 18:35).* The Lord's gentleness in Ruth made her great.

While most men are attracted to a woman's physical appearance at first, a good man wants a gentle and kind woman who can be a safe place his heart can trust. The passing beauty of a pretty face is a bonus to the inner beauty that lasts well beyond those years.

Beloved, God wants us to nurture the beauty in our hearts because He knows that outward beauty diminishes with time. Still, a woman who defines herself by her likeness to the Lord will possess the incorruptible beauty that never fades.

YOU ARE
BEAUTIFULLY MADE

I WILL PRAISE YOU, FOR I AM FEARFULLY AND
WONDERFULLY MADE; MARVELOUS ARE YOUR
WORKS, AND THAT MY SOUL KNOWS VERY WELL.
(PSALM 139:14)

WHEN WE TALK ABOUT INNER BEAUTY, all women can agree that this is something we can all achieve, but not every woman believes she is beautiful on the outside.

Many women struggle with feeling inadequate, average, not pretty enough, or not pretty at all. We all have things we wish we could alter or enhance. It is our nature as women to want to look beautiful. However, more often than not, women seek to change their appearance for the wrong reasons: to fix something they think is broken, ugly, or not as pretty as the other women they see.

Social media has made this problem even worse. Beauty has been redefined to focus on superficial, outward attractiveness only. As a result, women are under pressure as never before to look well put together and made up all the time.

Some women even alter their appearance so you can't recognize them when they are not done up.

The problem is not in wanting to look beautiful; it's the comparison and the self-loathing that result from not accepting ourselves and believing that we are already beautiful.

> *Your perception determines how you see yourself.*

We can become vain when we don't balance our desires to look beautiful with what God says about beauty. Unfortunately, some women take their efforts to an extreme and make idols out of their desire to live up to the world's standard of beauty.

Everything God made is beautiful. Everything God created is good (see Genesis 1:31). If you can't look in a mirror and see your God-created beauty, despite what you perceive as flaws in your height, weight, skin, or hair, perhaps you need to reconsider all the wonder and awe God put into forming you.

David was amazed when he thought about God's attention to detail when forming him, not just his spirit but also his body and outer frame. He said,

"How precious also are Your thoughts to me, O God! How great is the sum of them! If I

should count them, they would be more in number than the sand" (Psalm 139:17-18).

Beloved, you have to believe that you are beautiful. It is easy to do if you don't conform to the world's superficial beauty and perfection standards. Your perspective determines your perception.

If you look at yourself through the eyes of God's love and His thoughts toward you, you will see yourself as God sees you, beautifully and wonderfully made, "perfectly imperfect," as some like to say.

If you look at yourself through the eyes of your perceived defects and take in the negative things others may say about you, you will see yourself as hopelessly flawed. It's essential to embrace the beauty of your body, face, and features, to look in the mirror and like what you see. Not because you finally have "the look" that someone else defined as beautiful, but because you believe God gave deep thought to every detail when He formed you.

However beautiful a woman may be on the outside, her countenance is the most important part of her outer beauty because her countenance is a reflection of her heart. Your countenance will either draw people to you or turn them away.

Boaz was a righteous and wealthy man. He also had many women servants. I'm sure finding a wife wasn't a problem for him. However, he wanted a woman who had two-fold, lasting beauty. Ruth had it, and so do you.

I believe Ruth was beautiful because Boaz warned his men not to bother her. However, Ruth's outward

> *It's important to embrace the beauty of your body, your face, and your features, to be able to look in the mirror and like what you see.*

beauty was a complement, not a distraction, from her inner beauty. As Christian women, our appearance should be the same.

I love to put on pretty clothes and get dressed up. However, it's not how much make-up we wear or our clothes, but the Christ-like character we display that draws people to us.

It doesn't matter how pretty you are; a bad attitude will eventually push people away from you, but a pleasant attitude makes you stand out.

YOUR GARMENTS
ARE BEAUTIFUL

AWAKE, AWAKE! PUT ON YOUR STRENGTH, O
ZION; PUT ON YOUR BEAUTIFUL GARMENT. FOR THE
UNCIRCUMCISED AND THE UNCLEAN SHALL NO
LONGER COME TO YOU. SHAKE YOURSELF FROM THE
DUST, ARISE. LOOSE YOURSELF FROM THE BONDS OF
YOUR NECK, O CAPTIVE DAUGHTER OF ZION!
(ISAIAH 52:1–2)

I LOVE THE BOOK OF ISAIAH because it is a
picture of Christ's redemption of His Beloved
Bride—the church. That's us! When Isaiah spoke
those words to the children of Israel, though they
were God's chosen people, they had been lured
away into a place of physical and spiritual bondage because of their desires to be more like the
people around them who did not have a relationship with the one true God.

Though God loved, accepted, and called
them beautiful, they were still drawn away by

their lust. Their once-beauti-
ful garments had become
the filthy garments of sin
and captivity. God, in His
loving-kindness, still offered
them a way back to Him
and new beautiful gar-
ments to change into.

> **Changing our garments isn't a one-time deal. We have to continually return to God to be cleansed because we live in a fallen world.**

That is what Christ does
for us, His Beloved Bride. He
takes our filthy rags and
gives us a wardrobe full of
new beautiful garments
meant to be worn on our hearts: righteousness,
peace, and purity, regardless of what we wore in
the past.

The only catch is: before you put on your
beautiful garments, you have to take off your old
garments.

> Jesus put it this way, "No one tears a piece
> from a new garment and puts it on an old
> garment. If he does, he will tear the new, and
> the piece from the new will not match the
> old" (Luke 5:36).

Changing into your beautiful garments means
doing away with the cares and sins of the world
and putting on Christ. It's washing clean from
your past with the Word of God and clothing your
heart with His promises. This lets the world know

you have chosen to be known as God's daughter and no longer want to be identified as being "of the world."

Changing our garments isn't a one-time deal. This is obvious in the story of the children of Israel. We must continually return to God to be cleansed because we live in a fallen world with outside influences. The beautiful thing is, however, that we can always return, and God is always willing to take us back and wash us clean. He cleanses our hearts from sin, heals what is broken in us, and we truly become beautiful instead of settling for just being pretty.

Ruth changed the garments of her heart long before she married Boaz. She took off her old identity and any fears and anxieties about her future and put on the beautiful garments of the heart fit for one of God's daughters. When Boaz met Ruth, he called her "daughter" because she was clothed in her new identity (Ruth 2:8).

Beloved, the lies you're wearing, the sins, the things holding you in bondage to a false identity and telling you that you can't be the beautiful woman God created you to be, know that by faith, you can take them off, and step into the beautiful garments God created for you.

YOUR WORSHIP
IS BEAUTIFUL

OUT OF ZION, THE PERFECTION OF BEAUTY,
GOD SHINES FORTH.
(PSALM 50:2)

ZION IS a physical location in Jerusalem, where David set up his stronghold when he became king over all of Israel, and the spiritual place where God is enthroned in worship and praise. Geographically, it is known as the City of God and the City of David.

When David erected the tent of worship in Zion, the tabernacle of Moses was still in place, but the ark of God and the glory of God were long gone. It had not been in the tabernacle for some twenty years. The Philistines had captured it under Saul's rule but did not keep it. They sent it to one place and then another because God struck down each group who had it due to their ungodly and idol-worshipping practices.

When David finally went to get the ark of God, it was at Abinadab's house (1 Samuel 7:1). Instead of putting the ark back in the tabernacle of Moses, David erected another tent in Zion, the city of David. The glory of the Lord that had departed from the tabernacle of Moses filled the tent once again. (Find the full story in 1 and 2 Samuel.)

It wasn't the tabernacle or the law that made the glory of the Lord depart; the law of the Lord is perfect (see Psalm 19:1). It was the condition of men's hearts and their worship of idols that did it. Moses was a friend of God (see Exodus 33:11). But many of the people he led drew near to God with their mouths, but their hearts were far from Him.

Jesus said:

The hour is coming, and is now here, when the true worshipers will worship the Father in spirit and truth, for the Father is seeking such people to worship him. God is spirit, and those who worship him must worship in spirit and truth. (John 4:23–24)

We are called to worship the Lord in spirit and truth. Truth is the reality of God's Word working in us. His Word is Spirit. When we allow His Word to work in us, the reality of His Spirit starts working in us.

Spiritual worship is a life lived for God, making our hearts and homes places where His presence can dwell. It is an authentic expression of love toward God for the revelation of who He is.

David, a man after God's heart, built a place for true, spiritual worship in Zion. The Old Covenant Zion points to the reality of

> *The completion of His beauty shines through our authentic worship of the living God.*

spiritual Zion being the church in the New Covenant.

Hebrews 12:22–23 says:

But you have come to Mount Zion and to the city of the living God, the heavenly Jerusalem, and to innumerable angels in festal gathering, and to the assembly of the firstborn who are enrolled in heaven, and to God, the judge of all, and to the spirits of the righteous made complete.

It is from this place of worship, the heavenly Jerusalem, the spiritual Zion—that the completion of His beauty shines through our authentic worship of the living God, the Beautiful One.

Ruth lived a life of spiritual worship. She did not come to know God through the law and religion. She came to God through her relationship with her mother-in-law and the relationship she built with Boaz, then the Lord himself.

The truth was written in her heart. She sought to please the Lord with her life and her actions. Her worship was spiritual and authentic.

Because Ruth worshiped the Lord in spirit and truth, the completion of beauty could shine through her, and she was granted enrollment in heaven. Beloved, this is the beautiful worship the Father desires from you.

YOUR INHERITANCE IS BEAUTIFUL

THE LORD IS MY CHOSEN PORTION AND MY CUP; YOU HOLD MY LOT. THE LINES HAVE FALLEN FOR ME IN PLEASANT PLACES; INDEED, I HAVE A BEAUTIFUL IN-HERITANCE. (PSALM 16:5–6)

THE WORD PORTION means *allotment*, and the word *cup*, in this context, can be understood as a form of sustenance or provision. The word *lot* means destiny. The lines are the boundaries that have been prearranged and preassigned to us. The Lord holds our destiny. He is the one who measures our boundaries and appoints our portion.

When Ruth chose to follow Naomi, she gave up her right to choose whom she would marry. This left Ruth at the mercy of others. But she chose to make the Lord her portion, and her decision changed the course of her destiny.

Women are often left at the mercy of others. Women get divorced and have to start over with little or nothing. Women get abused and then discarded. Women are left to raise alone children they did not make alone.

> **The Lord holds our destiny; He is the one who measures our boundaries.**

Women are often left wondering if they will ever enjoy the reality of a beautiful inheritance. But those of us who choose to make the Lord our God have a Redeemer who loves us. *"In Him we obtain an inheritance" (see Ephesians 1:11).* When you choose to make the Lord your portion, He will lead you into the beautiful inheritance He has prepared for you.

In the story of Martha and Mary, the two sisters who were friends of Jesus, Mary chose to make the Lord her portion, but Martha was distracted with serving:

> Martha welcomed him into her house. And she had a sister called Mary, who sat at the Lord's feet and listened to his teaching. But Martha was distracted with much serving. And she went up to him and said, "Lord, do you not care that my sister has left me to serve alone? Tell her then to help me." But the Lord answered her, "Martha, Martha, you are anxious and troubled about many things, but one thing is necessary. Mary has chosen the good portion, which will not be taken away from her." (Luke 10:38-42)

The Lord loved both Martha and Mary. However, Martha had forgotten what was most important, as many of us do at times. Perhaps you do the same thing, serving the Lord out of gratitude for everything

> *He will lead you into the beautiful inheritance He has prepared for you.*

He does for you. However, the Lord desires that we do more than serve Him. He wants a personal, intimate relationship with each one of His daughters.

Mary chose to sit at the Lord's feet first and make Him her chosen portion. By doing so, He became her provision in everything she needed. By taking time out of her day to sit at the Lord's feet first, Mary was storing up treasures: an inheritance for herself in heaven. This "good portion" has eternal value and cannot be taken away.

Like Mary, Ruth allowed the Lord to instruct her, and in doing so, He led her into her destiny and gave her a beautiful inheritance of eternal value. When she married Boaz, Ruth gained a place among the women in the lineage of the Messiah. She was also blessed with earthly rest from her labors and worries and given peace and wealth.

She had access to everything Boaz had, and all he redeemed from her husband's family was at her disposal. With her blessings, she was able to be a blessing to Naomi.

As women, we do a lot to care for our families and other people. Unfortunately, we sometimes take on too much responsibility, and the important things get neglected.

> *The lie the devil wants us to believe is this: our "good works" can replace the time that should be spent as a necessity with the Lord.*

The lie the devil wants us to believe is this: our "good works" can replace the time that should be spent as a necessity with the Lord.

The truth is that much of what we do is unnecessary and won't lead to the life we crave because even if we have everything we want in this world, Jesus is the only One that can truly satisfy a heart created to be filled with His presence.

Beloved, Jesus has an inheritance for you that cannot be taken away. Our portion is with the Lord, within the boundary lines He sets for us. He has given everything we need that pertains to life and godliness in the form of seed promises.

When we choose to spend time with the Lord, He helps nurture those seeds so we can see the manifestation of everything He's given us become a reality in our lives:

> *His divine power has granted to us all things that pertain to life and godliness, through the knowledge of Him who called us to His own glory and excellence, by which he has granted to us his precious and very great promises, so that through them you may become partakers of the divine nature, having escaped from the corruption that is in the world because of sinful desire. (2 Peter 1:3-4)*

Peter had experience with stepping into a divine inheritance. He also had to step out of who he was before becoming who God created him to be. He was a passionate apostle with great faith but untamed flesh. He matured in his faith when he learned to supplement it with good character.

Peter wrote:

> *For this very reason, make every effort to supplement your faith with virtue, and virtue with knowledge, and knowledge with self-control, and self-control with steadfastness, and steadfastness with godliness, and godliness with brotherly affection, and brotherly affection with love. For if these qualities are yours and are increasing, they keep you from being ineffective or unfruitful in the knowledge of our Lord Jesus Christ. (2 Peter 1:5-8)*

Peter listed all the character traits Ruth possessed and cultivated throughout her life. As Peter laid hold of the promises of God in the presence of the Lord and moved forward in the purposes of God and his calling, his fleshly nature gave way to the law of Spirit, and the seeds of God's promise were able to produce the fruit.

Like flowers in the springtime, the promises of God will bloom into the beautiful inheritance God laid up for you when you make Him your portion and learn to supplement your faith with godly character.

QUESTIONS

1. What does God desire for each of His daughters?
2. How is vain beauty produced?
3. What is twofold beauty?
4. How does the Bible define the heart?
5. How does bitterness grow in our hearts?
6. Has bitterness ever taken root in your heart? If so, how did you uproot it?
7. How can bitterness contaminate those we have influence over?
8. How can we make sure that doesn't happen?
9. How can we nurture the beauty of the heart?
10. Why is gentleness associated with inner beauty?
11. What problems does focusing only on external beauty create?
12. What are the dangers of seeing yourself through what others say about you?
13. Why is it important to see yourself as beautiful?

14. As Christian women, what should our appearance be?

15. What do we have to do before we can put on our beautiful garments?

16. What does it mean to take off your old garments?

17. What does it mean to put on your beautiful garments?

18. Why isn't changing our garments a one-time event?

19. What is spiritual worship?

20. How do we offer the Lord spiritual worship?

21. What does Zion represent?

22. How does God's beauty shine through your worship?

23. Who measures our boundaries?

24. What happens when we choose to make the Lord our portion?

25. What lie does the devil want us to believe about good works?

26. What are we supposed to supplement our faith with? Why?

PRAYER

Father, thank you for making me altogether beautiful and forming me fearfully and wonderfully. Help me remember to embrace my physical beauty and nurture the beauty you planted in my heart.

Help me to reflect your beauty in all my ways and to put on the beautiful garments you prepared just for me. Help me to know I'm free to go back to you whenever I need to change my garments so that I step fully into the identity of beauty you prepared for me.

Let my worship be a spiritual and beautiful reflection of you. Lord, thank you for my beautiful inheritance. Help me to make you my portion and trust you to lead me into the fullness of my destiny, in Jesus' name, Amen.

MINDSET

MEASURE

MISSION

STEP IN

Now that you understand God's love, acceptance, and beauty, it's time to step into His L.A.B. and be the woman He created you to be so you can possess your inheritance and live victoriously.

But first, you have to change your mindset– the standards you use to measure yourself and understand your mission in life as God's daughter.

MINDSET

A MINDSET is an established set of attitudes and beliefs held by someone. Think of your mind as a file cabinet with several folders filled with instructions for processing all of life's issues. These instructions are mindsets.

Mindsets are formed when certain attitudes and beliefs are embraced and allowed to take root in your heart and mind. Most mindsets are rooted in things we were taught and experiences that happened early in life. Your mindsets affect the way you process things, your emotions, your decision-making, and your judgment. The way you respond to life's issues, whether good or bad, is determined by your mindset.

Erroneous mindsets originate in false thoughts, the lies of the devil, and flawed information that, at times, is passed off as truth, tradition, or principle. However, any mindset that does not align with the word and will of God is erroneous.

> *Your mindsets affect the way you process things, your emotions, your decision-making, and your judgment.*

Erroneous mindsets enforce themselves through reasoning, arguments, and the opinions of the carnal mind, which is set against the knowledge of God and His will for you.

The devil uses wrong mindsets to limit and control people and to keep them stuck in the same cycles of defeat. You can have the right mindsets in one area of life and be bound by a stronghold in another.

For example, you can believe that God loves you and, therefore, that you are worthy of love from others. On the other hand, if you do not believe that God made you beautiful, you may never like what you see when looking in the mirror.

When wrong mindsets are embraced, allowed to take root, and acted on, they become strongholds — opinions and attitudes raised against the knowledge of God. (2 Corinthians 10:5)

Strongholds control your reasoning and thinking so that the truth concerning God's will for you cannot break into your thoughts and affect how you process information. Strongholds keep you conformed to the world's way of doing things so you never experience the transformation God desires for you. Strongholds must be pulled down and destroyed (2 Corinthians 10:4–6). You do this by challenging your wrong thinking and mindsets with the truth in God's word.

You must pay attention to your thoughts to change your wrong thinking and mindsets. Then capture and replace any false thoughts with God's word, accepting as true what He says about you and meditate on God's word in whatever area you need transformation.

Philippians 4:8 says:

Whatever is true, whatever is honorable, whatever is just, whatever is pure, whatever is lovely, whatever is commendable, if there is any excellence, if there is anything worthy of praise, think about these things.

When you believe what God says about you, you begin to see yourself as He sees you, and this is what transforms you and produces God's perfect will in your life. God wants you to change your thinking to prove His good, acceptable, perfect will in every area of your life.

Ruth could have let the mindsets of her past rule her future, but by faith, she welcomed the truth, and it transformed her life.

God is no respecter of persons. If He did it for Ruth, He will do it for you. Allowing the truth to change how you think about love, acceptance, and beauty will transform your life.

REPLACE
LIES WITH TRUTH

ON A BLANK PAPER, skipping a line after each, write the truth: what God says about you.

Next, list any negative, self-defeating thoughts contrary to what God says about your relationship with Him, your identity, your calling, and His plans for you under each truth you wrote. Read each negative thought aloud. Then put a line through each negative statement and read aloud only what God says about you.

Finally, on a clean piece of paper, only write what God says about you. Use your list of truths as your weapon to tear down strongholds and renew your mind. Use your list against the enemy when he whispers his lies to you.

MEASURE

FOR WITH WHAT JUDGMENT YOU JUDGE, YOU WILL
BE JUDGED; AND WITH THE MEASURE YOU USE, IT WILL
BE MEASURED BACK TO YOU.
(MATTHEW 7:2 NKJV)

A MEASURE IS THE DEGREE, level, or standard by which we judge ourselves and others and apply our understanding. The standards with which we measure ourselves, others, and the issues of life come from our mindset. Therefore, having the godly mindset when making judgments and decisions about yourself, your life, and other people is important.

The standards you use to judge others will be the same measurement used to judge you. When you judge others using the wrong measure, you expose what you believe about yourself and God.

The degree to which you believe God's word is true is the degree to which it will become real to you. If you believe you are beautiful and worthy of love and acceptance, you can love, accept, and find beauty in others.

You won't value others as God wants you to if you believe you are of little worth. However, if you believe you're worthy of every good and perfect gift from God, you will naturally begin to think that other

> *Your measure is the degree, level, or standard by which you judge.*

people are, too. When you feel beautiful and worthy of love and acceptance, you can form authentic relationships with people who see those same things in you, who will help you step fully into your destiny like Ruth did for Naomi and Boaz for Ruth.

Many women measure things by the world's standard. They allow what they hear and see on social media and entertainment to cloud their judgment about love, acceptance and beauty. They let them affect their definition of their worth.

Maybe you used to judge yourself, your situations, and others by the world's standards. It's time to make God's Word your standard. God's standards are His love for you and the people around you. His standards are acceptance of those who make Him their God and compassion for those who are different. Everything and everyone God makes is beautiful, so His standard for beauty is that we look not only at the outward appearance but also at the heart of people and see the beauty in everything and everyone He created. When you look at other women, know that we are all beautiful in the eyes of the One who made us all.

MISSION & MOTTO

Each season, having a mission statement and a motto will help you fulfill your purpose.

A mission summarizes what you are called to do to fulfill God's purpose for you season by season. A motto is a summary of your guiding beliefs. Mission statements and mottos only work if you commit to living by them.

Mission statements and mottos only work if you commit to living by them.

MISSION

FOR WE ARE HIS WORKMANSHIP, CREATED IN
CHRIST JESUS FOR GOOD WORKS, WHICH GOD PRE-
PARED BEFOREHAND, THAT WE SHOULD WALK IN
THEM.
(EPHESIANS 2:10)

YOUR MISSION and your purpose are connected, but they are not the same. Your purpose
is the "expected end" God planned for you before you were born (see Jeremiah 29:11). Your
mission is the good works God calls you to do you
were called to do to fulfill your purpose on. Your
mission can and does change season by season
but your purpose remains the same. Knowing
your mission and actively pursuing it leads to fulfilling your purpose.

A personal mission statement is a statement
that defines your values, who you are, and what
God has called you to do each season. A personal mission statement can be used to guide
your decisions and help you stay focused on your
purpose season by season.

If Ruth had a personal mission statement during the season she moved to Moab, I believe it

would have been "To provide for Naomi and my-self and be her friend." My mission is to "know God, be a good mom, serve others, and preach the gospel."

To create your personal mission statement, answer the following questions:

- What does God want to do in and through your life?
- What do you believe is His ultimate plan for you? It does not have to include church ministry. It can be to be a good wife and mother. To be a good friend. To provide food for the poor. To write books. It can be more than one thing.
- What gifts, talents, and abilities has God given you to do that?
- Who do you have a heart for, and who are you called to serve?
- What are you passionate about?
- What is your vision for your life?

To write your mission statement, look for the common theme in your answers, including your motto, core values, beliefs, and principles. Then write a statement that expresses what and how you will do the one or few things God has called you to do this season that align with what He wants to do in and through your life. Once you create your motto for this season, you will have the foundation to develop your mission state-ment.

MOTTO

YOUR WORD IS A LAMP TO MY FEET AND A LIGHT
TO MY PATH. (PSALM 119:105)

A MOTTO summarizes your guiding beliefs and values that help shape your behavior as you try to live up to the mission it represents. It is a concise and consistent core principle that reinforces a concept you already believe.

When confusion or negative thoughts arise, rehearse your motto to remind yourself of the direction you want your life to go.

Creating a motto will encourage your faith and keep you on the right path. Your motto may change as you go through different seasons in life.

My motto was "Joy is strength" (Nehemiah 8:10) during the season I went through my divorce.

Rehearsing my motto helped me live my life around the truth it represented. God's joy became my strength in that tough season, and I kept an attitude of grace and gratitude.

> **Rehearse your motto to remind yourself of the direction you want your life to go.**

Ruth's name means friend or neighbor. When Naomi chose to call herself Mara during that bitter season of her life, Ruth embraced the meaning of her name.

If Ruth had a motto during that season, I believe it would have been *"A friend who sticks closer than a sister"* (Proverbs 18:24, *emphasis added*). She was such a good friend to her mother-in-law that Naomi's friends said she was better to her than "seven sons" (Ruth 4:15).

If you had a motto for this season of life, what would it be?

To create your motto, look for a scripture that expresses the values, principles, or beliefs you want to live your life around. Look for things that stood out in your mission statement. Write a statement encompassing the values, principles, or beliefs you want to direct your path this season in a few words or verses. You may need to try out different mottos until you have one that feels right.

Your practice of intentionally living by your mission and motto statement will help reinforce your godly mindset. It will encourage you to be the woman God called you to be and continue doing what He called you to do season by season.

Beloved, God wants to fulfill His plans for you. He wants you to reach your destiny. Having a personal mission statement and a motto is like having a compass to help you navigate each season. Every day you endeavor to live up to things they represent brings you closer to fulfilling your purpose.

Other Books by Krista Pettiford

Called Out
A Blueprint For Walking In Your Calling With Clarity, Confidence, and Courage

Surrendered Balance
Daily Living for the Modern Christian Woman

Contact:
Website: kristapettiford.com
Email: info@kristapettiford.com